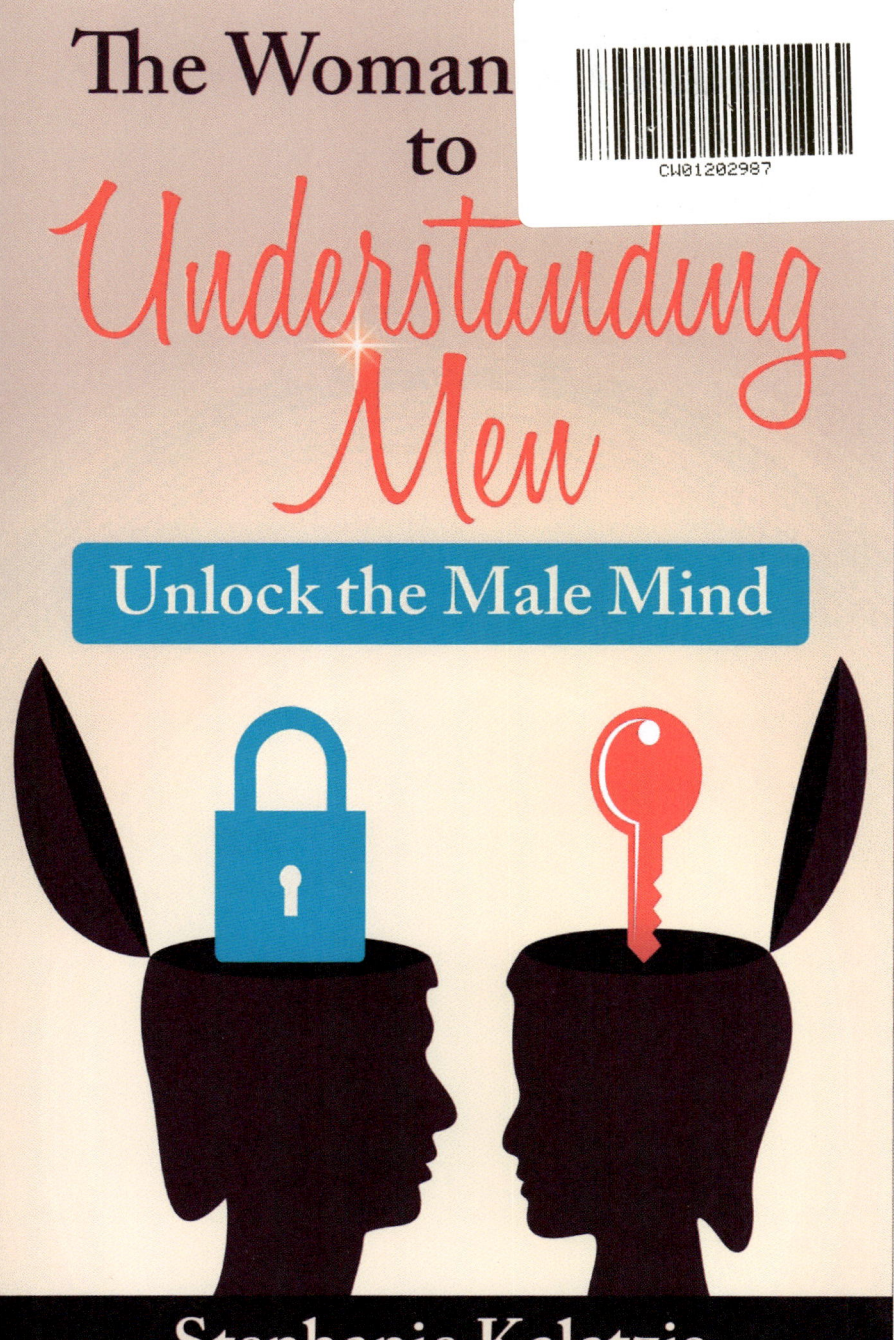

A Woman's Guide to Understanding Men

Unlock the Male Mind

Stephanie Kalatzis

Copyright:

Copywright@2015 Stephanie Kalatzis. All rights reserved. Recording of this publication is strictly prohibited and any storage of this document is not allowed unless with the written permission from the author and publisher.

Addressing my beloved readers:

Thank-you for downloading my e-book "A Woman's Guide to Understanding Men". Written in a straightforward and down to earth manner, this guide aims to help you women understand the workings for the male mind, and enables you all to have a quick understanding of the critical aspects of the book without feeling burdened by an difficult jargon contained within it.

YOUR FREE GIFT

http://www.kindlefreebies.com/go/understanding-men-2

As a special Thank You for downloading this book – I have put together an exclusive 50 tips to understanding men, that, if followed, is guaranteed to help you achieve the most satisfying relationship with your man.

TABLE OF CONTENTS

FREE GIFT

INTRODUCTION

BETWEEN THE EARS – HOW MEN THINK

ONE FOR YOU, ONE FOR ME- WHAT MEN EXPECT

HIT THE SPOT- HOW TO REALLY SATISFY A MAN

BOYS WILL BE BOYS- ACTIONS AND BEHAVIORS OF MEN

FINAL THOUGHTS

1
INTRODUCTION

"There are no perfect relationships. It's how we accept the imperfections that makes it perfect."

A relationship between a man and a woman is a complex thing to understand. A woman's ideal man possesses some, if not all, of the following qualities -to be rich, handsome, trustworthy, masculine, understanding, and above all, respectful. Settling back down to reality, women must accept the fact that there is a difference between ideal and real men. Now although, there are men out there who come close or even exceed these ideals, these are not the norm – rather, exceptions to the rule.

This eBook is written for female readers looking for an inside peak into the thoughts and processes of men. Whether you are currently single, in a relationship, engaged, or have been married for decades, the principles and tips presented in this book can be used as a tool to better your odds in sustaining a loving relationship with a man.

Please note that this eBook has not been designed to teach women how to control or change men. It serves the sole purpose of teaching women the ways of men, and provides instructions on how to alter your own behavior in ways that are better reciprocated by men. By communicating and behaving in ways that are recognizable to men, women will naturally create better outcomes for the relationship in times of disagreements and discrepancies.

This eBook acknowledges that the responsibility of sustaining a successful relationship cannot be placed on one partner alone. It is not the sole responsibility of the woman to ensure the livelihood of her relationship. Compromise and mutual effort is highly regarded. This eBook is just one half of the puzzle, to give women the tools necessary to either just maintain, fix-up, or completely restore the structures of her relationship. Don't worry, there'll be a whole other book created for men. Let's just worry about what you can do for your relationship first. For all problems in life, we must always first look within us for a solution before looking at and blaming our environment and others. By the end of this eBook you'll know whether there is anything more you can do for your relationship, or whether you do what you're already doing, but just do it a little differently.

This eBook will explore and explain the thought processes of men, their attitudes and behavior, and their true satisfaction triggers. Hope you have a wonderful experience reading this eBook. So, let's proceed to the first chapter. Happy Reading!

2
BETWEEN THE EARS – HOW MEN THINK

"Here's all you have to know about men and women: women are crazy, men are stupid. And the main reason women are crazy is that men are stupid." – George Carlin

Sitting across from him, watching him scoff down his dinner, have you ever wondered what he thinks about himself? His life? You? Or even the food? Behind that eating machine is your man, who just like you has his own needs, his preferences, his passions, his strengths, his weaknesses, and his own style. However, unlike you, each of these segments are thought about at a completely different wave length to women.

First thing you need to know understand is that men are simplistic, commonsensical creatures. If it looks happy, it's happy. If it looks grumpy, it's grumpy. If you say you're fine, to him you're fine. In general, men have a very rational outlook on life and logical approach toward solving problems. Think of a man as a carrot – a carrot has a very thin layer of skin that, at times, doesn't even need to be peeled, it is pretty much ready to cook and eat. Women, think of yourselves as an onion – an onion has numerous layers that need to be peeled away before it is ready to cook and eat. Onions are more delicate and require greater preparation. And because onions think like onions, they expect carrots to think like onions as well – that is mistake number one.

Men, typically, do not read too deeply into a situation like women. However, do not make the next mistake of assuming simple means dumb or inferior. Men owe their simplicity to their beliefs that "what you see is what you get".

Men often have difficulty decoding messages from women with hidden meanings or unspoken emotions. Just as it is difficult for a person to read someone's tone through emails or texts, so too is it for a man to read what you are really feeling. You will hardly hear a man ask you: "how do you feel, *actually*?" – as for him, asking: "how do you feel?" he believes, will produce an honest response from you. Men typically do not twist their words and call it as they see it – something that is all too uncommon with women.

There are also some physiological reasons that explain the differences between how men and women think. Known as the '7 year maturity gap', neurologists worldwide have studied and tested the brain development differences between men and women, particularly when entering adulthood during puberty. Throughout puberty, there are noticeable physical changes transforming the body on the outside, but more discreetly, there are hidden neuro-chemical and hormonal changes transforming the body on the inside. It is believed that female hormones mature faster and are therefore easier to regulate compared to male hormones.

Other researchers have found that parts of the frontal lobe - responsible for problem-solving and decision-making, and the limbic cortex - responsible for regulating emotions, are larger in women. This information is validated by the fact that male drivers under the age of 25 pay greater car insurance premiums and excess fees. For men however, the parietal cortex - which is involved in space perception, and the amygdala - which regulates sexual and social behavior, are larger.

Women need to understand and accept the impact this difference in development has on men and their thought processes. These differences in processing thoughts create differences in the expectations held by men compared to women.

What may be deemed as realistic for you may not be as realistic for him, keep that in mind.

3
ONE FOR YOU, ONE FOR ME– WHAT MEN EXPECT

"Treat a man as he is and he will remain as he is. Treat a man as he can and should be and he will become as he can and should be." – Stephen R. Covey

Honesty in communication

One of the biggest expectations a man places on a relationship and his partner is honesty in communication. A man expects his woman to give honest, direct answers to all his questions. He expects simple truths without any omissions or fleecing.

Women tend to hound men for their lack of communication skills or their lack of overall willingness to communicate – fair point. However, if you notice your man freely communicating with his friends, family, team-mates, or co-workers, then you must reflect on what is different in the communication channels between you and him, and them and him. Men often expect their woman to communicate like the others but are often disappointed by the complexity to which women impose on basic communication. Frustration from these bad encounters leads to blame and criticism toward one another which quickly disinterests the man, who would rather not communicate than be criticized or blamed again.

Women need to take from the learning's of the previous chapter and understand that men are simple. Any communication you want to engage in with your man should be as clear and unambiguous as possible. Strive for free-flowing communication, however avoid being critical. Patience is a must in these situations, as you won't always get it right first time round. Men expect women to be open and say exactly what they feel, so do it. If you avoid hesitation and say exactly what you think, you'll find your man more responsive which will frustrate you less. And you'll find yourself better expressed which will teach your man more about what you're thinking and feeling. This will preserve the sanctity of the relationship in the long-run.

Roles of each gender

Traditionally, the expectation of men has been to hunt, provide for, and physically protect their loved ones, whilst women have been expected to nurture, raise, and emotionally protect their loved ones.

Most men typically still expect this level of responsibility however, obviously, these traditional expectations have become harder to maintain with the changing times. In today's day and age we begin to see more of these roles and expectations intertwine between the two genders. Due to growing costs of living, women have been required to enter the workforce to generate higher family income, consequently, men have had to adopt greater domestic responsibilities.

By now sharing the responsibility of providing for the family, a man's self worth will be diluted. His innate obligation to provide will be conceded, and will cause him to compensate this loss of responsibility by demonstrating greater masculinity and dominance. A man has a certain level of pride that he feels he needs to uphold and will do everything in his power to maintain the image of his version of an ideal man (a provider).

A man's ego is hurt when he feels he is not providing for his loved ones. Women need to understand that this mentality is ingrained in the heads of all men. To avoid hurting your man's ego further, you need to give him greater responsibility, or at least perceived responsibility, in other decisions that impact the both of you. Simple things like deciding where to go out for dinner, what movie to watch, or even what to name the dog, will all create a greater sense of self-worth for the man. This doesn't mean you hand over all decision-making power to him, all that is required is that you assure him he still plays a major role in all decisions being made, and that his opinion is valued by you.

Lastly, men expect equality within the relationship. Fair division of responsibilities and duties is key for this equality. The perfect balance is needed for this to work as too much responsibility on him will have him feeling used and taken advantage of, whereas too much responsibility on you will have him feeling worthless and disposable.

Be like his mother..sometimes

The first woman a man meets is his mother. She is the one who typically nurtured him, helped raise him, and taught him emotionally. She is the one who cooked for him, who ironed is shirts, and the one who cleaned up after him. She is his first symbol of love. You should aim to fulfill these qualities and expectations and be like his mother in this way.

She is also the one who *should* have taught him how to become independent and do all of this crap on his own! If you have got yourself a man who has acquired this independence, then lucky you! If, however, you aren't so lucky, then you must tread carefully. If your man has not acquired this independence then it is difficult for him to change his expectations. He will expect you to do everything his mother did for him – and of course, this can be frustrating. If you are frustrated – consider these tips of advice:

1. Find a man who is independent. (Much easier for the single women reading, a lot harder to do if you are committed to the man you have - see step 2).
2. Stop doing everything for him! If you are constantly doing everything he expects, you are teaching him that his expectations are fine by you.
3. Slowly offload the different tasks and jobs you do for him one at a time (note: offloading all of your duties at once will put him into a state of shock, panic, and retaliation).

4. Be sure to maintain positive communication throughout the entire process – there is to be no blame or anger placed on him, simply express the contributions you make in the relationship compared to his. Even explain how, if he were to do the ironing or washing every now and again, it would give you more time to do other things for him, like prepare snacks for when his friends come over, or give you more energy for more frequent sex – that'll grab his attention!

Minimize platonic contact

A platonic friend is a very close male friend that a woman has. Their relationship is strictly "just friends" and usually never involves anything sexual– usually. Platonic friends are a big warning sign for most men. To men, platonic friends are seen as a dick in a glass case – break glass in case of an emergency! In your man's head that platonic friend is your plan B, your escape shoot, and he will do whatever he can to stop that. Typically, men do not have platonic friends - put simply, these women are just women they haven't slept with yet. Group this with their ego driven, protective nature, you can see why men would be intimidated and irritated by other men swooping in on their prize – you.

This is a very delicate situation you must always approach head-on and with full disclosure. If you are keeping ties with very close male friends once you enter a relationship with your man, your man will expect you to fully disclose:

- Your history with this friend – Were you ever more than friends? Did you ever hook up?
- His relationship status – He wants some reassurance that that friend is satisfied with his own woman, and to know that that relationship is stable and long-term.
- The depth of your friendship – He wants to know what is normal between you and that friend. Does he see you naked? Do you flirt with one another? How much respect does he have for your relationship?
- And whether or not you ever exhibited greater feelings toward him? – Another history based questioned, but one you should be dead honest about.

Some men are so against these platonic friends that they will give you an ultimatum – him or your platonic friend. This is a rarity, but it occurs more often than you would guess. The best way to combat this is to genuinely reassure him he has nothing to worry about, and to provide him with as many updates as you can on any contact you make with your platonic friend. It will put your man at ease and you will build up his trust one brick at a time.

Do, however, try your best to look at the situation from his perspective. Put yourself in his shoes and don't do anything you wouldn't want him to do with a female platonic friend. If you feel your platonic friend is crossing some blurred lines, be frank and be fair. If you value your relationship with your man, you should have no problem flicking this friend to the curb. If he is getting in between your relationship, perhaps an ultimatum will serve you best. Sometimes you can't have your cake, and eat it too.

Your independence

If you expect your man to show signs of independence, the same will be expected of you. Men want to be with women who see a man as a companion, a partner in crime. Men do not want women who only want a man who can satisfy her emotional and materialistic needs. Men do not want shallow women, rather, women who uphold their own set of values and independence. A man innately wants to provide everything for his woman, but only for a woman who doesn't expect it. Men never want to feel they are being used. Men like active, secure and confident women.

His space and his friends

A man's own space is one of his biggest expectations, and at the same time, one of the most unspoken expectations. Understanding this expectation alone will most definitely put you in his good books.

A man cherishes the time spent with his loved one, but he expects her to maintain a happy balance between the time spent together, and time spent apart. Men expect their women to have their own networks of friends who they can spend time with, particularly when men want to spend time with their friends. A man expects his woman to give him his own space and own time with his friends and his hobbies.

Usually the sense of humor of your man will change when he's around his friends. One of the minor expectations men have of women is to play it cool and go along with the joke. Sometimes your man will crack an inside joke (a joke that requires specific prior knowledge or experience), which you will not understand. In those times, you need to play it cool and ask him about the context when they are alone. Approaching it this way instead of calling him up on it at the time makes the whole moment less awkward and takes away any chance of you being judged or laughed at by his friends. Ideally, your man wants his friends to see you as "a cool chick" – a woman who can go with the flow and isn't on his case wanting to know the meaning behind everything he says and does. To his friends, this will be interpreted as clingy. The last thing your man wants is for his friends to think you're clingy!

It is expected that women understand the length and history of some of his friendships. Some of his friends he shares childhood memories with. These friends may have been with him for as long as either can remember. If you deem any of these friends as a bad influence or a worry, it is expected you tread carefully when bringing up these accusations to your man. Going in too strong or too blunt in these types of situations may have irreversible effects on the trust your man instilled with you.

The worst thing you can do is make him choose between you and his mates. Both of you play an equally important role in his life. When he chooses one, he does so with great difficulty. Men try their best to be fair and distribute their time evenly. A simple solution for these moments of uncertainty is for him to follow through with whichever plans were made first. If on Monday you asked him to go shopping with you on that Friday, and his friends ask him Thursday to see him Friday night, it would be right for him to go shopping with you. But, if the second invitation offered was perishable (could not be postponed or repeated) – for example, his friends scored tickets to their favorite childhood band's last ever show - then it would be reasonable for him to make an exception to the rule and ditch your shopping plans. In this case, he would expect for you to be understanding and offer alternatives – such as going shopping another time or taking one of your girlfriends shopping instead.

4

HIT THE SPOT – HOW TO REALLY SATISFY A MAN

"Every man needs two women: a quiet home-maker, and a thrilling nymph" - Iris Murdoch

To kick start this topic, we don't have to look any further than the expectations outlined in the previous chapter. Before digging deeper, first consider the expectations discussed earlier. They were: honesty in communication, roles of each gender, being like his mother..sometimes, minimizing platonic contact, achieving your independence, and respecting his space and his friends. Do you accept all these expectations? Are they fair enough? Do you meet or even exceed his expectations? And if not, why? Is it because his expectations are unreasonable or because you are unwilling? These are answers you need to answer, and fast, if you want to truly satisfy your man.

Remember, men are simple creatures. They know what makes them happy, and if someone is making them happy they will continue contact with that person, if they are not happy they will move onto someone who will.

Meeting his expectations are just scratching the surface of peak satisfaction. Many say the sure shot way to a man's heart is through his stomach and his balls – meaning, to really satisfy a man, all you need is to feed him good food and give him great sex. Men may be simple, but not *that* simple. Although these means are extremely effective, there are still plenty more boxes you must check off on his satisfaction list.

In addition to the aforementioned, below are several other criteria that make up the rest of your man's satisfaction checklist. Do your best to tick off as many of these points:

Listen to him – Continuing on from his expectation of honesty in communication, the key to satisfying your man is truly listening to him. There is nothing more frustrating for a man than when his simple message gets over-analyzed or taken out of context. Men, generally, are far better at getting to the point. They do not beat around the bush. Do your best to decode his message in its most literal form.

Encourage him to share more about himself and to open himself up to you. This may be a tough ask for new relationships, but still a necessary one if you want peak satisfaction. You should be aware of his desires, likes, dislikes, weaknesses, strengths and achievements.

Don't put him down, lift him up - Continuing on from the 'roles of each gender' section in the previous chapter, aim to provide moral support for all his ideas, projects and goals. Let him have the initiative. By doing so, his diminishing role as the sole provider will be compensated in the most productive way. If he wants to build that new garden shed or fix that hole in the wall, let him. Don't tell him he can't do anything. What's more, don't ever suggest for him to call 'the guy' for that. Already battling his own perceived deficiencies, the last thing your man needs is to have you suggest another guy come and fix the problem he can't. It is one of many forms of emasculation.

Understand that emasculation is a man's most dreaded feeling. Emasculation is any action that makes a man feel less masculine – it has the effect of depriving him from his male strength or role, and may make him feel weaker or less effective. This is a sure way of putting your man down. Emasculation can take many forms – the most blatant forms of emasculation come by way of comparing him (unfavorably) to others based on the size of his member, or on how long he lasts between the sheets. These are direct strikes at his manhood, and have the potential of being irreversible. Other forms of emasculation include comparing him based on his level of income, the car he drives, belittling what he does for a living, or even the amount of women he has been with. Less direct forms include, but are not limited to, asking him for help then doing it your way, yelling or fighting in public, or micromanaging everything he does.

To uphold your man's satisfaction, try be conscious of the things you say or do that may emasculate him in any way. Always build him up, and try feed his ego small portions - just as you would that goldfish in the bowl on the kitchen counter. Offer him daily compliments that acknowledge his masculine attributes. If your man is very active or goes to the gym regularly, drop lines that boost his confidence – lines like: "wow, your arms are looking bigger" or "your stomach is looking really trim, have you been running more?". If he performs exceptionally well in the bedroom, make sure you show your appreciation by telling him directly. Something along the lines of: "you were amazing last night, I slept like a baby, and today I feel so energized, thank you!" Having him hear your words of gratitude, particularly about touchy subjects like his sexual performance, will not only tremendously satisfy him, but also inspire him to uphold your level of satisfaction too. Just remember, the more your man feels like a man, the more fun he will have treating you as his lady!

Acknowledgment –After addressing all the things that emasculate your man, acknowledgement covers all the points that help restore your man's masculinity, confidence, and ultimately - satisfaction. A woman should appreciate and acknowledge as many of the efforts made by her partner – no matter how minor or insignificant they seem at the time. Appreciate the small initiatives made by your man. It's as simple as treating a dog when you ask it to sit. Acknowledgement is a man's reward for when he puts in the effort. Unnoticed or unappreciated gestures will quickly teach a man that his effort is pointless and worthless. If you see him putting in the effort, make sure he knows that you know.

Acknowledgement particularly goes a long way in instances where you, the woman, receive some sort of success or award. Wherever possible, and without lying, try link up one of his efforts to some of your own personal success. For example, if you receive a good mark on a college paper, attribute some (even miniscule) amount of your success to a conversation he had with you on the topic, or an idea that he gave you. Another example, if you receive a bonus from work for outstanding service or exceeding targets, link your success to any of the efforts you have noticed from him at home – for instance: saying something like: "without your extra help around the house, I don't think I could have performed so well at work" or "it was our talks in bed late at night that kept me motivated and focused at work".

The only way any form of acknowledgement will work is if it is genuine. Be sure you mean absolutely everything you say. That is why it is only required to attribute the tiniest portions of your success to his efforts – because it is most likely true. For him, doing more around the house will, in most cases, give you that extra slice of energy at your job. The hard part of acknowledgement is paying attention to those deeds you usually miss. The only way you can successfully acknowledge your man's efforts is to know what they are. Do spend the time to remember the little things he does so as to ensure your moments of acknowledgement are as sincere as can be.

Do what he likes with him – Most people form bonds based on mutual interests, but it seems in relationships, men and women seem to stray away from each other's. Wherever possible, try embrace his interests. Gaining an appreciation for his interests is a great way of pleasantly surprising and impressing him. If he enjoys running, try running with him. If he is a musician, try jamming with him, or even just humming along. If he is obsessed with sports, things like remembering the names of his favorite sports players, or the name of his team's home ground will go a long way. Not only will it satisfy him, but it will also score well with his friends.

However, just make sure you know the difference between the cool girlfriend who can name the captain of the team and the clingy girlfriend who keeps intruding the man cave. In most cases, all that is required to satisfy your man is for you to spit out the absolute basics of his hobbies. This may require a little bit of research on your end, but hey, you must obviously be prepared to research, seeing as how you have gone out of your way to read this book.

Let's get physical, physical – Physical intimacy plays an important role when trying to satisfy your man. It is no secret, men are sexual creatures, and with all this sexual energy, it must be expelled somewhere. Understanding your man's sexual appetite will better equip you with the knowledge you need to deliver satisfaction. Knowing things as simple as what time of the day he prefers to have sex, how many times a week he likes to have sex, and at what intensity, will all help you piece together a perfect recipe for his pleasure.

Another tip for sexual satisfaction is to treat his eyes before his member. Compared to women, men are extremely visual creatures who rely on visual cues for their arousal. Women tend to rely much less on visual cues and are better stimulated by seductive words and thoughts. Feel comfortable enough to have sex with the lights on – even if it is dim light. There is nothing less appealing for a man, than a self-conscious woman who is too embarrassed to treat his eyes. If he wasn't physically attracted to you, he wouldn't be with you, embrace your body and flaunt your assets. Find the perfect balance between teasing him and giving in to him, between you controlling the tempo and him controlling the tempo. Mix it up, but always try to incorporate his favorites.

Being physical doesn't just revert to sex. Basic, small gestures such as holding your partner's hand while walking, placing your hand on his thigh while sitting next to each other, or placing an arm around your partner's shoulder while sitting on the couch all convey the message of love to your partner. All these little physical points of contact reassure your man that he is cherished and loved. It is necessary to work out your man's ideal affection level so as to ensure you are not over doing it or making him feel uncomfortable – particularly when in the company of others.

Smooth sailing– Based on their simple nature, men appreciate nothing more than a drama-free relationship. With so many drama based television programs geared toward women, it is fair to say women seem to attract and enjoy more drama than men. Shows like *The Desperate Housewives, Keeping up with the Kardashians, Jersey Shore* and *The Real Housewives of New Jersey* all portray drama as a basic commodity, and at often times, a necessary component to any worthwhile relationship. The reality of these shows (pun intended) is that they are oozing drama because drama, arguing and bitching gets more eyes glued to television screens. Sadly, most people are more entertained by negative, drama-filled stories than they are by positive, up-lifting stories. Understand that unless you're a celebrity that can sell their life story, a drama-filled relationship will not do you any good.

A major part of truly satisfying your man is developing techniques to better control your urges to react dramatically. When you are stressed with something like work or your own family, it becomes very easy to find fault in the relationship and point the finger at your partner for every little thing at that time. This is unfair, and at most times, illogical. Behaving like this will only cause bigger problems.

The best way to avoid such turbulent situations is taking a step back and performing an analysis that distinguishes things that genuinely stress you out or making you unhappy, and the things that only seem to make you unhappy when you are already stressed. For example, yelling at your man because he left a dirty glass on the coffee table without a coaster usually wouldn't bother you, but after a long day at work and with the new boss breathing down your throat, you seem to kick up a fuss over that dirty glass.

5
BOYS WILL BE BOYS–ACTIONS & BEHAVIORS OF MEN

"Men do not quit playing because they grow old; they grow old because they quit playing."– Oliver Wendell Holmes, Sr.

It is said a man is judged by his character. That character is determined by his behavior.

Any behavior your man exhibits in front of, or toward you, can be explained with one of the following intentions. They are:

- To gain your attention or impress you – particularly during courtship or when you are not in an exclusive relationship.
- To gain your acceptance or approval – perhaps for you to approve of him, or his family, or his lifestyle choices. Many of the behaviors used to gain your attention and impress you will carry over to this intention once you are in a relationship with him.
- To keep balance in his own life – he will exhibit certain behaviors sometimes as a way to achieve his perceived level of balance in life. This may feel as if he is distancing himself from you as your idea of balance won't be the same as his.
- To indicate displeasure – If there is an abundance of the behaviors used to keep balance in his life, it may have an

underlying message: He is smothered and overwhelmed by the relationship.
- To impart dominance or feed the male ego – to hide or improve some shortcoming or weakness he has (could be physical or emotional).
- To gain the acceptance or approval of his friends - Because that's what his friends have taught him is right/normal. The male ego is most heavily influenced by companions and associates. It is the wolf pack mentality – he must be like the others in the group so as to avoid being perceived as weaker or singled out for being different.

It is difficult to talk about the intentions of behaviors for all men, as all men will attribute their own actions and behaviors to their own personal intentions. That is what makes them who they are.

With that in mind, below is a list of different qualities, traits, and behaviors men will exhibit throughout their adult life. Of course, not every item on this list will be relevant to your man.

This eBook has done its best to segment these different behaviors based on their typical intentions.

Please note that some of these behaviors may not even be present in your man. Also, please note that some of these behaviors may not have those exact intentions or may even have several intentions you may not be aware. But be sure that you can bring every one of these behaviors down to at least one of the six intentions.

Behaviors to gain your attention or impress you – particularly during courtship or when you are not in an exclusive relationship.

- Grooming and personal hygiene - His hair is neatly styled. His shirt is tucked in. He smells delicious. His shoes are polished. And his breath is as fresh as a winter's day.
- Punctual – He doesn't keep his lady waiting. He is first to arrive. He's the man with the plan for the evening.
- Cooking – He dazzles you with his knowledge that stems far beyond the realms of fried eggs and instant noodles.
- He works out – He hits the gym. He's in good shape. He is physically active. It is scientific knowledge that physically fitter men perform much better in the bedroom.
- A reader – He woos you with his love for the paperback. There is something attractive about a man who can consume information through mediums other than television.
- Romantic – Sends flowers. Sends good morning and good night messages. Puts effort into his plans with you. Gives you small gifts.
- Chivalrous– He opens the door for you. Pulls out your chair. Offers his jacket if you are cold. Offers to pay for the initial meals and activities.
- Family orientated – Shows you his nurturing side through his interaction with his family. Gives you a snippet into what a potential future might look with him.

- Funny – One of the main reasons men try to be funny is because laughter extinguishes awkward silences. Another reason is that a smiling, laughing, happy woman is one of the most attractive sights a man will ever see. For him, a happy wife is a happy life!
- Play hard to get – Men understand the notion of wanting what you can't have. That is why, at times, men offer some women less attention. This is usually done as a ploy to manipulate the behavior of women who are perceived as being more sought after or women who appear less interested. Men go by the simple rule: Treat them mean, keep them keen. They will do jusssssst enough to keep you keen on him, and after that, will try have you believe you cannot have him.

To gain your acceptance or approval – perhaps for you to approve of him, or his family, or his lifestyle choices - Many of the behaviors used to gain your attention and impress you will carry over to this intention once you are in a relationship with him – this is because you may have set a standard or expectation of him which he has to uphold. He will most likely not play hard to get when already in an established relationship with you.

To keep balance in his own life - He will exhibit certain behaviors sometimes as a way to achieve his perceived level of balance in his life - This may feel as if he is distancing himself from you as your idea of balance won't be the same as his. These behaviors include, but are not limited to:

Sports – If you have to keep a score, he watches it. The idea of competition accelerates him. Whether he's watching it, playing it, or talking about it, it distracts him from the stresses of his everyday life.

Television – Documentaries, movies, news, sitcoms. They all serve the same purpose as sports – a distraction to life.

Hobbies – Collectibles, Cars, Home Improvement, Gardening, Hiking, Fishing, Hunting. Once again – creates distraction and breaks up his stressful routine.

Bars and Clubs – Sometimes sports, television and hobbies aren't enough to take the edge off. Sometimes alcohol is required to create some balance. There is nothing wrong with an occasional beverage.

To indicate displeasure - If there is an abundance of the above behaviors used to keep balance in his life, it may have an underlying message: He is smothered and overwhelmed by the relationship.

Too much of any of these 'life balancing' behaviors is a warning sign for his dissatisfaction. Monitor any changes in these particular behaviors – and look within yourself for any reasons why he is requiring more balance in his life. Are you expecting too much of him? Are you giving him his space? – One of the expectations covered in chapter two.

To impart dominance or feed the male ego – Many of these behaviors aim to hide or improve some shortcoming or weakness he has (could be physical or emotional). They help cover any insecurities he does not want known by you or others. Such behaviors include:

- Showing off – Whether it is his muscle car that goes from 0 – 60 in who cares seconds, or whether it is the half a tone he can bench press at the gym. Showing off with these types of 'accomplishments' are all intended to impart dominance over other men who he feels he needs to measure up against – and win.
- Being protective – Bordering on possessive, men treat their woman like a precious jewel. They have the instinctive nature to be the provider and protector. Like a caveman protecting his family from a wild predator, your man protects you from the dangers he believes in – in most cases, other men who prey on taken women. This protective nature allows a man to showcase his dominance to not only you, but to the other men around.

To gain the acceptance or approval of his friends - How many times have you heard your girlfriends, or even yourself, say something along the lines of: "He's just so different when he's with his friends".

Whether you are with him around his friends or he is with them on his own, this distinct change in behavior is quite normal and stems from the nature of the relationship he has with his friends. Reflect on yourself for a moment; how different do you behave around your parents compared to your co-workers or compared to your girlfriends? Each different personal relationship a person has with another grows and creates its own direction with its own set of norms, rituals, traditions, and its own formalities. Most men have formed relationships with their friends that do not incorporate romance or love as part of their norms. Knowing this, your man has developed the neat skill of transitioning his behavior between you and his friends. This does not mean he loves you any less or that he is embarrassed of you in any way. When he is without you, the transition in behavior can be the result of many factors. They include;

- Monkey see, monkey do – His behaviors are based on what his friends have taught him is right or normal. Usually he does not talk about you because his friends don't talk about their partners. Many men use their time with their friends as an escape. It is their way of achieving balance in their life too. It is one of the few places they can come and remove the stresses of their lives and divert their attention to simpler things like football, beer, and food. Remember – men are simple. Us women are complex creatures who send men's brains into overdrive just to stay on par with us. It's like revving your car's engine to the red – the car then needs time to cool off before it can go again.

- The wolfpack mentality – He feels that he needs to behave and act in a way that resembles his friends' behavior and actions so as to avoid being perceived as weaker or being singled out for being different.
- Braggers beware – In many instances, the reason your man will not bring you up in conversation is because he believes his friends will perceive it as bragging. Your man may not feel comfortable talking about his happiness to friends who are unhappy or seeking a relationship. If he senses envy from his friends in any way, he may feel uncomfortable expressing his blessings, particularly ones as good as you!

6
FINAL THOUGHTS

"Love doesn't make the world go 'round. Love is what makes the ride worthwhile."

Having covered and explained how men think, what their expectations are, what truly satisfies them, and why they act and behave the way they do, you should now have a better understanding of men. Following the recommendations and ideas proposed by this eBook will give you the insight you need to, not only establish a stronger communication channel with your man, but also, create a more open and understanding connection with him.

Use the lessons from this eBook as a stepping stone toward solidifying your relationship and future with your loved one. Yes, this eBook was heavily one-sided and focused only on you – the woman – changing, or improving. But, this is because this eBook was created only for the eyes of women. Now that you have read your part, have your partner read his part in the corresponding book within this series – 'Understanding Women'. Once both of you have read your part, hopefully a stronger understanding and appreciation for one another's differences will be established.

Bear in mind that no matter how much you learn about your partner through this learning experience, the learning should never stop. Life is not static, it is constantly changing and taking up new shapes and forms. The same applies with people. Although many of our traits stay with us, there are plenty that evolve or simply fade away. To maintain a healthy, loving relationship, both must avoid the trap of thinking they know everything there is to know about their partner. Understanding the subtle changes in your partner will secure your relationship in the long run. You should remain curious about one another, always acknowledging and speaking about the differences in thought processes and expectations. In the end, you want to be each other's best friend – someone who you can console with in times of hardship.

> "A successful relationship requires falling in love several times, but always with the same person."

If you've enjoyed reading the e-book, kindly leave me an objective review so that I can further improve on my future guides. Once again thank you for reading.

Printed in Great Britain
by Amazon